THE ALL-TOO-ROMANTICS
(Les Romanesques)

*A comedy in three acts
by Edmond Rostand*

English version by Thom Christoph

GENGE PRESS

Genge Press
29, West Park
Minehead, TA24 8AN
UK

All rights reserved. No part of this publication may be reproduced, stored in a retrieval system or transmitted at any time or by any means, electronic, mechanical, photocopying, recording or otherwise, without the prior permission of the publisher.

© 2024 Thom Christoph

For performance rights please contact:
gengepress@btinternet.com

ISBN 978-0-9549043-7-1

Foreword

Les Romanesques, a lighthearted play in three acts, was Edmond Rostand's first success in the theatre. First performed on 21st May 1894, it was warmly received by the audience at the Comédie-Française, the state theatre, and confirmed the twenty-six-year-old author's desire to make writing in verse for the theatre his life's work. (He always wrote in verse, claiming that it came more naturally to him than prose.) After writing two poetic plays for the renowned actress Sarah Bernhardt, Rostand received the chance to write a play about – and immortalise – a character in French history he had always admired, Cyrano de Bergerac.

Rostand described *Les Romanesques* as "a *Romeo and Juliet* with a happy ending". The "all-too-romantics" of the title are Percinet and Sylvette, who live next door to each other and fancy themselves modern incarnations of Shakespeare's star-crossed lovers. They meet in secret at the wall separating the gardens of their feuding fathers, hoping wistfully for an end to the hostilities, which does in fact come – from a source the young people could not have suspected – just in time for the first-act curtain. They become engaged.

But such an unrealistic victory for young love would have taxed even Rostand's joyous romanticism, and in the two succeeding acts Percinet and Sylvette each experience, with the help of a swashbuckling swordsman named Straforel, a sobering taste of the real world, which paves the way for them to a more mature, but no less loving, outcome.

Soon after its premiere, *Les Romanesques* was translated into a dozen languages and has remained a favourite with amateur groups ever since. It was the inspiration, in 1960, for *The Fantasticks* by Tom Jones and Harvey Schmidt, which then went on to become the world's longest running musical.

One sees in *Les Romanesques* many of the qualities that would later serve Rostand so well in *Cyrano de Bergerac*: his witty and lyrical verse; his gentle humour at the expense of his characters; his stagecraft; and his ability to convey serious ideas in a lighthearted way. Straforel, with his swagger and eloquence, is very much a forerunner of Cyrano.

The extant English versions of *Les Romanesques* are now over a century old and bear the stamp of their time. Thom Christoph, who has already translated this play into German and Catalan, believed it was time for a new one, and we are delighted that he now offers us *The All-Too-Romantics* in his deft blank verse.

—Sue Lloyd, Genge Press
Author of *The Man Who Was Cyrano*

The persons of the play:

SYLVETTE, *an all-too-romantic young lady*

PERCINET, *an all-too-romantic young man*

BERGAMIN, *Percinet's father*

PASQUINOT, *Sylvette's father*

STRAFOREL, *a swordsman*

A GARDENER

A NOTARY

FOUR WITNESSES

Non-speaking roles: swordsmen, musicians, sedan-chair porters, torchbearers, etc.

The play is no doubt set somewhere in the South of France during the 18th or 19th century, certainly prior to 1894 (when the play was premiered); in any case, the costumes must be pretty.

The All-Too-Romantics
Act One

The stage is divided in two by an old wall that is covered with moss and garlanded with wild climbing plants. Next to the wall are two benches, one on either side. Stage right shows a corner of Bergamin's garden; stage left, a corner of Pasquinot's garden.

When the curtain rises, Percinet is seated atop the wall with a book on his lap, out of which he is reading aloud to Sylvette, who is standing on the bench on the left, leaning on the wall with her elbows and listening attentively.

Sylvette:

Oh, Percinet, how truly beautiful!

Percinet:

Yes, isn't it? Then Romeo answers, saying:
(Reading:)
'It was the lark, the herald of the morn,
no nightingale. Look, love, what envious streaks
do lace the severing clouds in yonder east.
Night's candles are burnt out, and jocund day
stands tiptoe on the misty mountain tops.
I must be gone…'

Sylvette, *imagining she has heard a noise:*
Shh!

Percinet, *after listening for a moment:*
                No one's there!… My dear,
don't play the timorous bird who'd flee her perch
at any little noise! Hear Juliet speak:
'Yon light is not daylight, I know it, I;
it is some meteor that the sun exhaled
to be to thee this night a torchbearer

and light thee on thy way to Mantua.
Therefore stay yet; thou needst not to be gone.'
He says: 'Let me be ta'en… be put to death.
I am content, so thou wilt have it so.
I'll say yon grey is not the morning's eye;
'tis but the pale reflex of Cynthia's brow.
Nor that is not the lark whose notes do beat
the vaulty heav'n so high above our heads.
I have more care to stay than will to go.
Come, death, and welcome! Juliet wills it so.'

SYLVETTE:
Oh, no, don't let him speak so, or I'll cry…

PERCINET:
All right, we'll close our book until tomorrow
and let your Romeo live another day.
(He closes the book and looks about the gardens.)
This lovely spot might well have been designed
for basking in the Bard's inspiring verses.

SYLVETTE:
Oh, yes, his verses are magnificent,
and murmuring leaves accompany them well
and make a fitting backdrop. But for me,
what makes those lines most touching, Percinet,
is your melodious voice – and how you read them!

PERCINET:
You naughty flatterer!

SYLVETTE, sighing:
                Oh, those poor lovers!
How cruel their fate, how meanly they were treated!
(With another sigh:)
Ah! I was thinking…

PERCINET:
What?

SYLVETTE, quickly:
             Oh no, it's nothing…

         PERCINET:
You had some thought – and suddenly went pink!

         SYLVETTE, quickly:
No, no!

         PERCINET, wagging a finger at her:
       You're fibbing – and your eyes betray you.
I see what you were thinking of…
(Lowering his voice:)
                      … our fathers!

         SYLVETTE:
Perhaps…

         PERCINET:
       And of the hatred that divides them!

         SYLVETTE:
You're right; the thought of them distresses me
and often makes me weep when I'm alone.
When I returned from convent school last month,
my father pointed to your father's garden
and said to me, 'My child, there lies the lair
of Bergamin, my mortal enemy.
You must avoid that scoundrel and his son.
Give me your word, or else I shall disown you,
that you'll forever be their enemy,
for they and all their clan have always loathed us!'
I gave my word… You see now how I keep it!

         PERCINET:
Didn't my father make me swear as well
that I would hate you evermore, Sylvette?
And yet I love you!

SYLVETTE:
Heaven save my soul!

PERCINET:
I love you, child!

SYLVETTE:
But that's a sin!

PERCINET:
A grave one…
and yet it's so. The more they try to stop me
from loving you, the greater my desire.
Sylvette, come, kiss me!

SYLVETTE:
Never on your life!
(She jumps off the bench and moves away from the wall.)

PERCINET:
You love me, though!

SYLVETTE, faintly shocked:
What are you saying?

PERCINET:
Child,
although your heart may still rebel against it,
it would be wrong to doubt it any longer.
I'm saying what you said yourself, Sylvette,
comparing, as you did, Verona's lovers
to two young people here.

SYLVETTE:
No, I compared…

PERCINET:
Well, you compared our fathers, yours and mine,
to those of Romeo and Juliet.
That's why the two of us *are* Romeo
and Juliet – and why we're so in love!

And I defy – despite their bitter hatred –
my father, Bergamin, as Montague
and Mr Pasquinot as Capulet!

    SYLVETTE, moving a bit closer to the wall:
We love each other, then? But, Percinet,
how ever could that come about so quickly?

        PERCINET:
Who knows how love is born – or why or when?
I often saw you passing by my window…

        SYLVETTE:
I saw you too…

        PERCINET:
    Our eyes spoke secretly.

        SYLVETTE:
One day, there, near the wall, as chance would have it,
I was collecting nuts…

        PERCINET:
        And I, by chance,
was reading Shakespeare, there. And Fate contrived…

        SYLVETTE:
A sudden breeze came up and blew my ribbon
to your side of the wall…

        PERCINET:
        And to return it,
I quickly climbed our bench…

    SYLVETTE, climbing back onto the bench:
        And I climbed ours!

        PERCINET:
And since then, every day I wait for you.
My heart starts fluttering when I hear your laughter
behind the wall, which always culminates

in your emergence through the quivering vines.

> *SYLVETTE:*

Since we're in love, we must become betrothed.

> *PERCINET:*

That's just what I was thinking.

> *SYLVETTE, solemnly:*

        It's to you,
last of the Bergamins, that now is plighted
the last descendant of the Pasquinots!

> *PERCINET:*

A noble madness!

> *SYLVETTE:*

    Future generations
will speak of us!

> *PERCINET:*

    'Two all-too-tender children
of all-too-ruthless fathers!'

> *SYLVETTE:*

        But – who knows? –
perhaps the hour has come when Heaven wishes
to see their hatred quelled – by us?

> *PERCINET:*

        I doubt it.

> *SYLVETTE.*

But I trust Providence to find a way;
already I've envisioned five or six
quite possible conclusions.

> *PERCINET:*

      Really? Tell me.

> *SYLVETTE:*

Suppose – I've read such things in several novels –

the Prince comes passing by one day… I run
to plead with him and tell him of our love
and of our fathers' hatred – after all,
a king once wed Ximena to El Cid!
The sympathetic Prince sends for my father
and Bergamin, makes peace between the two…

Percinet:

… and marries us!

Sylvette:

Or else it works out so,
as in 'The Princess in the Donkeyskin':
you're languishing in sorrow, close to death;
a stupid doctor says he cannot save you…

Percinet:

My frantic father asks: 'Son, what d'you want?'

Sylvette:

You say: 'I want Sylvette!'

Percinet:

And thus his pride –
his stubborn pride must yield!

Sylvette:

Or here's another:
some ageing duke has seen my portrait somewhere
and fallen hopelessly in love with me;
he sends a splendid cavalier to win me
as duchess for his lord.

Percinet:

And you say: 'No!'

Sylvette:

The duke's enraged, and one night, while I'm strolling
about our garden, lost in dreams of you,
I'm kidnapped!… I cry out!

P̄ercinet:
                            And suddenly
I spring up right beside you, grasp my sword
and, with a lion's fearlessness, do battle,
quickly dispatching…

Sylvette:
                        … three or four assailants.
My father rushes forward to embrace you,
so moved that, even when you name yourself,
he feels compelled to give me to my saviour.
Your father, too, is then so proud of you
that he consents as well.

Percinet:
                            And we all live
together in the greatest happiness!

Sylvette:
And none of that seems too far-fetched now, does it?

Percinet, hearing a noise:
Shh! Someone's coming!

Sylvette, forgetting herself:
                Kiss me!

Percinet, kissing her:
                                And this evening,
when they ring vespers, will you meet me here?

Sylvette:
No!

Percinet:
    Yes, you will!

Sylvette, disappearing behind the wall:
                Your father!
(Bergamin enters. Percinet has jumped down from the wall. Sylvette remains invisible to Bergamin.)

Bergamin:
                              Once again
I catch you at your daydreams, all alone,
here in this corner of the garden?

Percinet:
                                   Father,
I love to sit here – it's my favourite corner!
The bench is sheltered by the falling vines.
Such graceful vines they are, too, don't you think?
Festoons of a most striking arabesque!
I find the air is purer here!

Bergamin:
                                 The air
is purer by the wall?

Percinet:
               I love this wall!

Bergamin:
This wall has nothing I'd call lovable.

Sylvette, aside:
He doesn't see it!

Percinet:
             But it's marvellous,
this ancient wall, with grass along its crest,
covered with russet vines and verdant ivy,
with long, mauve clusters of wisteria,
with honeysuckle – and with Dutchman's-pipe!
This crumbling, hundred-year-old wall, whose cracks
have strange red hairs that dangle in the sun;
this wall, bestarred with pretty little flowers;
this wall, on which the moss has grown so thick
it makes a backrest for this humble bench,
as plush as that of any sovereign's throne!

BERGAMIN:
Tut-tut! Young pup, would you have me believe
you come here just to see the wall?

PERCINET:
                              Oh, yes!
I fancy even that the wall sees me…
(Turning towards the wall:)
… with smiling eyes, astonishingly blue!
Profound cerulean flowers, how you delight me!
Should ever tears impearl your chalices,
I'll make them vanish with a single kiss!

BERGAMIN:
You fancy that the wall can see you? How?
It's got no eyes.

PERCINET:
          But it's got morning glories.
(And he graciously presents one, hastily plucked, to his father.)

SYLVETTE:
My God, is he not clever?

BERGAMIN:
                              You're a blockhead!
But I know well what's making you so foolish.
(Percinet and Sylvette react with fright.)
You come here secretly – to read.
(He takes the book from Percinet's pocket, and looks at its spine.)
                              Hmph! Theatre!
(He opens it, then drops it with horror.)
In verse yet! *That's* what's fogged your brain! No wonder
you dream and mooch about – and can't be talked to!
That's why you blather over Dutchman's-pipe
and why you think this wall's got eyes of blue!
A wall need not be pretty – just secure.
I'll have this overgrowth of green removed,

-14-

which might be hiding any crevices,
and, to protect us from our brazen neighbour,
reface the wall, then plaster it with whitewash.
I'll garnish it with – no, not Dutchman's-pipe,
but sharp-edged glass shards wedged into the plaster
in tight battalion all along…

PERCINET:
Oh no!

BERGAMIN:
Oh yes! With glass shards all along the crest!

SYLVETTE and PERCINET, dismayed:
Ohh!

BERGAMIN, sitting down on the bench:
Come, let's have a chat.
(He gets up and moves away from the wall with a suspicious air.)
But wait!… For walls,
although they don't have eyes, may well have ears!
(He starts to climb onto the bench, a move which frightens Percinet; at the sound, Sylvette cowers behind the wall, making herself very small. But Bergamin gives up the effort after some old rheumatic pain wrenches a grimace from him, and he motions to his son to come up in his place and look around.)
See if some nosy parker…
(Percinet climbs deftly onto the bench. Leaning over the wall, he lowers himself to Sylvette, who immediately straightens up.)

PERCINET, aside to Sylvette:
Till tonight!
(Sylvette gives him her hand, which he kisses.)

SYLVETTE, in an undertone:
I'll come here when the church bell sounds for vespers!

PERCINET, in an undertone:
You'll find me here!

Sylvette, in an undertone.
I love you!

Bergamin, to Percinet:
Well?

Percinet, jumping to the ground; aloud:
There's no one.

Bergamin, reassured, sitting down again:
Now then, let's talk… My son, I want you married.

Sylvette:
Ay!

Bergamin:
What was that?

Percinet:
I didn't hear a thing.

Bergamin:
I heard a feeble cry.

Percinet, looking into the air:
Some wounded birdie…

Sylvette:
Alas for me!

Percinet, pointing vaguely:
There, high up in the trees!

Bergamin, picking up the threads:
And so, my son, upon mature reflection,
I've made a choice for you.
(Percinet walks away from him, going upstage, whistling. Bergamin gasps at this insolence, then follows his son.)
Now hear me, boy,
I'm adamant in this, and I shall force you…
(Percinet comes back downstage again, but still whistling.)
Stop whistling like some wretched blackbird, will you?

The woman's young and very rich – a jewel!

                PERCINET:
And what if I don't want your jewel?

                BERGAMIN:
                                How dare you!
(He raises his cane threateningly.)
I'll show you, you rapscallion!

        PERCINET, lowering his father's raised cane:
                               Father, springtime
has filled the bushes with the sound of wings,
and every woodland stream has pairs of birds
caressing one another…

           BERGAMIN, raising his cane again:
                              Don't be cheeky!

        PERCINET, lowering his father's cane again:
… all nature smiles, extolling April's advent;
the butterflies…

           BERGAMIN, raising his cane again:
                  You scapegrace!

        PERCINET, lowering his father's cane again:
                              … swarm the fields
to pollinate their cherished flowers, while Cupid…

                BERGAMIN:
You rascal!

                PERCINET:
        … sets all hearts ablaze with love –
and you would have me married out of *reason*?

                BERGAMIN:
Of course I would, you blackguard!

           PERCINET, in vibrant tones:
                            Never, Father!

I swear upon this wall – and hope it hears me! –
that I shall marry so romantically
that one could never read in any novel
of anything more hopelessly romantic!
(He runs out.)

      BERGAMIN, *running after him:*
I'll catch you!

       SYLVETTE, *alone:*
    I can almost understand
my father's hatred for that mean old –
(Pasquinot, her father, enters from the left.)

      PASQUINOT:
            Well?
What are you doing here, young lady?

      SYLVETTE:
           Nothing.
Just walking.

      PASQUINOT:
    Here, alone? But – you poor child! –
you're not afraid?

      SYLVETTE:
    I'm not a fearful person.

      PASQUINOT:
But I've forbidden you to approach this wall!
Dear, unwise girl, d'you see that garden there?
The hideout of my mortal enemy!

      SYLVETTE:
I know, Papa.

      PASQUINOT:
     And you expose yourself
to their insulting words, to…? Don't you know
what those malicious reprobates might do?

Were they to learn – that devil and his son –
that my dear daughter comes here all alone
to daydream… Oh, I shudder at the thought!
But I have plans to fortify this wall,
to armour it with bristling iron spikes,
so anyone attempting to surmount it
will be eviscerated and impaled.

SYLVETTE, aside:
He'll never do that; it would cost too much.
Papa's so frugal!

PASQUINOT:
Get inside!
(She goes out; he glowers after her.)

BERGAMIN, speaking to someone in the wings:
Deliver
this note at once to Mr Straforel!
(Pasquinot, hearing his voice, runs quickly to the wall and climbs up.)

PASQUINOT:
Hey, Bergamin!

BERGAMIN, doing the same:
Hey, Pasquinot!

(They embrace.)

PASQUINOT:
How are you?

BERGAMIN:
Not bad.

PASQUINOT:
Your gout?

BERGAMIN:
It's better. And your head cold?

PASQUINOT:
Not gone yet.

BERGAMIN:
Well, the wedding's in the bag!

PASQUINOT:
What?

BERGAMIN:
I was hiding in the undergrowth
and heard them talking. They adore each other!

PASQUINOT:
Hurrah!

BERGAMIN:
Our happy ending's now in sight!
(Rubbing his hands together:)
Ha! Look at us, a pair of widowed fathers:
me, with a son, whose too-romantic mother
christened him Percinet…

PASQUINOT:
A silly name!

BERGAMIN:
… you, with a daughter, starry-eyed Sylvette.
And what was our intent, our sole objective?

PASQUINOT:
To have this wall torn down…

BERGAMIN:
To live united!

PASQUINOT:
… and merge our two adjoining plots of land!

BERGAMIN:
Two shrewd old cronies…

Pasquinot:
> … and proprietors!

Bergamin:
And what was needed to achieve our goal?

Pasquinot:
> The marriage of our children!

Bergamin:
> Yes, their marriage!
But it would never work if they suspected
what we were planning: marriage by arrangement
could hardly tempt two such poetic ninnies.
As long as they were safely far away,
we kept our nuptial plans for them a secret;
but now, this year, they've both returned from school.
I realised that forbidding them to meet
would surely make them seek each other out –
and that a secret, guilty love would please them,
so I invented our dramatic feud!
You doubted such a gambit could succeed?
Well, all we have to do now is consent!

Pasquinot:
But how can we consent convincingly
without their growing wary? After all,
I did call you a reprobate, a bonehead…

Bergamin:
A bonehead? 'Reprobate' was quite sufficient.

Pasquinot:
But how do we explain our making peace?

Bergamin:
Aha! It was your daughter who suggested
the perfect stratagem. As she was speaking,
my plan took shape. They're meeting here tonight:
a rendezvous. First, Percinet appears;

then, when Sylvette shows up, some dark-clad men
spring out from under cover and abduct her.
She screams! My intrepid son runs after them
and skirmishes with them – a bit of swordplay;
they flee. You show yourself, then I arrive.
Your daughter's safe; her honour is intact.
Your joy's intense: you bless her valiant saviour
while brushing tears of gladness from your eyes.
I'm deeply moved. We pose – *tableau vivant.*

PASQUINOT:
Why, that's a stroke of genius! Truly – genius!

BERGAMIN, modestly:
Well… if you say so!… Hush! D'you see who's coming?
It's Straforel, the celebrated swordsman;
I wrote to him just now about my plan –
our kidnapping. He's just the man to stage it.
(Straforel, in an ornate swordsman's costume, appears at the back and advances majestically. Bergamin comes down from the wall and goes to greet him.)
Ah, Mr Straforel! I'm Bergamin,
and this is my good neighbour, Pasquinot.

STRAFOREL, bowing:
How do you do, sirs?
(As he rises, he is surprised not to see Pasquinot.)

BERGAMIN, pointing to Pasquinot astride the wall:
On the wall – up there.

STRAFOREL, aside:
Amazing stunt for one so ripe in years!

BERGAMIN:
Dear Maestro, does my plan seem…?

STRAFOREL:
Elementary.

BERGAMIN:
Of course, you're expert, agile…

STRAFOREL:
And discreet.

BERGAMIN:
The abduction's merely feigned, as is the combat?

STRAFOREL:
That's understood.

BERGAMIN:
I trust that all your swordsmen
are skilled – they mustn't hurt my boy. I love him –
my only child!

STRAFOREL:
I'll operate myself.

BERGAMIN:
Ah, very well! Then there's no need to worry.

PASQUINOT, aside to Bergamin:
Say, ask him how much it will cost!

BERGAMIN:
Dear Maestro,
what do you take for staging an abduction?

STRAFOREL:
Why, that depends on what you wish to pay;
abductions come at many different prices.
But if I understand your case correctly,
you shouldn't stint on cost. If I were you, sir,
I'd take our premium model – our First Class.

BERGAMIN, dazzled:
Ah! You have several classes?

STRAFOREL:
But of course!

Imagine, we've the Ordinary Abduction
– a simple hackney with two men in black –
it's not requested often. We've the Abduction
by Dark of Night; the Abduction in Broad Daylight;
the Imperial Court Abduction, full of pomp,
with powdered lackeys and a royal carriage
(an outside firm would bill you for the wigs),
perhaps with page boys, musketeers, equèrries –
as you may wish; the Abduction in a Post Chaise,
with two, three, four, five horses – there's no limit.
The Abduction in a Black Berline is surely
discreet, although for my taste rather sombre;
the Abduction in a Boat is most romantic,
but here, unhappily, you have no lake.
(In Venice we've lagoons – and gondolas!)
Abductions come with moonlight or without;
as moonlight's in demand, it's more expensive.
The Dire Abduction, in a thunderstorm,
with clanging swordplay, noisy stamping feet,
and men in broad-brimmed hats and slate-grey mantles;
the Rude Abduction; the Polite Abduction;
the Abduction Under Torchlight – very pretty! –
the Masked Abduction, an enduring classic;
the Abduction Pastorale, with chamber music;
the Abduction in a Portable Sedan Chair –
the newest, jolliest, most refined of all!

>BERGAMIN, *scratching his head, to Pasquinot:*

Well, what do *you* think?

>PASQUINOT:
>I don't know… And you?

>BERGAMIN:

Well, I think we should really push the boat out!
Imagination! Bits of everything!
The abduction should be…

STRAFOREL:
>Mixed? I can arrange it.

BERGAMIN:
Let's give our fantasts something to remember:
sedan chair, mantles, torchlight, music, masks!

>*STRAFOREL, taking notes on a notepad:*
For billing purposes, First Class with extras.

>*BERGAMIN:*

Agreed!

>*STRAFOREL:*
>I'll come back in a little while.
(Indicating Pasquinot:)
But I must ask the gentleman to leave
the garden gate on his side slightly open.

>*BERGAMIN:*
You needn't fear, you'll find the gate ajar.

>*STRAFOREL, bowing:*
Till later, gentlemen.
(As he is going out:)
>First Class with extras…

>*PASQUINOT:*
With all his airs, the great man took his leave,
but never named his price!

>*BERGAMIN:*
>It doesn't matter;
the deal is done. Now we can tear the wall down!
We'll have a single home!

>*PASQUINOT:*
>And in the winter
we'll only have one rent to pay in town!

BERGAMIN:
How beautifully we'll decorate the garden!

PASQUINOT:
We'll sculpt the hedges!

BERGAMIN:
Strew the paths with sand!

PASQUINOT:
Our monograms, in script made out of flowers,
will intertwine in every garden bed!

BERGAMIN:
I find this stretch of lawn a bit severe…

PASQUINOT:
A few glass gazing balls will perk it up!

BERGAMIN:
We'll have an ornamental pond for goldfish!

PASQUINOT:
We'll have a fountain with a dancing egg!
We'll have a garden stone!… Well, you old rogue,
what do you think of that?

BERGAMIN:
It's the fulfilment
of all our wishes!

PASQUINOT:
We'll grow old together!

BERGAMIN:
Your daughter's taken care of!

PASQUINOT:
So's your youngster!

BERGAMIN:
Ah, dear old Pasquinot!

PASQUINOT:
Dear Bergamin!
(They fall into each other's arms. Sylvette and Percinet come in suddenly, she from the left, he from the right.)

SYLVETTE, *seeing her father holding Bergamin:*
Oh!

BERGAMIN, *seeing Sylvette, to Pasquinot:*
It's your daughter!

PERCINET, *seeing his father holding Pasquinot:*
Oh!

PASQUINOT, *seeing Percinet, to Bergamin:*
Your son!

BERGAMIN, *in an undertone to Pasquinot:*
Let's fight!
(They transform their embrace into a hand-to-hand struggle.)
You ruffian, you!

PASQUINOT:
You wretch!

SYLVETTE, *pulling her father by the tails of his jacket:*
Papa!

PERCINET, *pulling Bergamin by the tails of his jacket:*
Papa!

BERGAMIN:
Leave us alone, you nuisances!

PASQUINOT:
He struck me!

BERGAMIN:
He insulted me!

PASQUINOT:
You reprobate!

SYLVETTE:
Papa!

BERGAMIN:
You miscreant!

PERCINET:
Papa!!

PASQUINOT:
You churl!

SYLVETTE:
Papa!!!

(The children manage to separate their fathers.)

PERCINET, *dragging his father away:*
Come back inside, Papa, it's getting late!

BERGAMIN, *trying to return to the fight:*
I'm raging still!
(Percinet leads him off.)

PASQUINOT, *trying to return to the fight:*
I'm foaming at the mouth!

SYLVETTE, *leading him off:*
It's growing cool – think of your rheumatism!
(Daylight is beginning to fade. The stage remains empty for a moment. Then, in Pasquinot's garden, Straforel enters with his swordsmen, musicians, etc.)

STRAFOREL:
The first star has appeared, and daylight's fleeing…
(He places his men.)
You, take your station there… you, there… you, there.
The hour of vespers now is close at hand,
and she'll appear just as the church bell rings.
Then I shall whistle…
(He looks at the sky.)
Ah, the moon – that's perfect!

Not one effect shall we have missed this evening!
(Examining the extravagant mantles of the swordsmen:)
The cloaks are excellent! Press on your cross-guard;
the blade should push the mantle back a bit.
(The sedan chair is brought in.)
Place the sedan chair, porters, in the shade.
(Calling into the wings:)
Torchbearers, don't come in until I whistle!
(The background becomes vaguely pink by the reflections of the torches behind the trees; the musicians enter.)
Musicians? There, with pink light in the background…
(He places them in the background.)
Be graceful, pliant, varied in your poses:
the mandolin should stand, the viol should sit –
as in the famous painting by Watteau.
(Sternly, to a swordsman:)
First Masked Man, careful how you walk – you're shambling!
(The swordsman corrects his gait.)
Ah, yes, now *that's* a swagger! Good!…
(To the musicians:)
                                          Musicians,
please tune your instruments – *pianissimo*.
(He masks himself. Percinet enters slowly. During the following, the night gets darker and the sky fills with stars.)

                     PERCINET:
I calmed my father down and stole away.
Daylight is fading, and the elder trees'
intoxicating scent floats through the air;
the flowers are disappearing in the half-light…

             STRAFOREL, *softly to the musicians:*
You may begin!

                    PERCINET:
            I'm trembling like a reed –
I wonder why!… Ah, soon I'll see Sylvette!

STRAFOREL, *to the musicians:*
Adagio amoroso!
(The musicians play softly until the end of the act.)

PERCINET:
This will be
our first nocturnal meeting… I feel faint!
The breeze is rustling like a silken gown.
My vision's blurred by tears; the flowers have vanished –
yet I can smell them all the more distinctly.
A single star now crowns that towering cypress.
Is someone playing music?… Night has fallen.
(The church bell tolls in the distance. Sylvette appears.)

SYLVETTE:
The church bell. He'll be waiting now.
(Straforel emits a shrill whistle and springs up in front of her; the torches emerge from behind the trees. Sylvette cries out:)
Ah!
(The swordsmen carry her off and quickly place her in the sedan chair.)
Help!

PERCINET:
Good God!

SYLVETTE:
Help, Percinet! I'm being kidnapped!

PERCINET:
I'm coming!
(He climbs over the wall, draws his sword, and fences with several swordsmen.)
There – take that! Take that! Take that!

STRAFOREL, *to the musicians:*
Tremolo!
(The strings raise a dramatic tremolo. The swordsmen flee.)

STRAFOREL, *exclaiming theatrically:*
Zounds! This youth's the spawn of hell!
(He draws his sword and engages Percinet in a duel. Suddenly his hand flies to his chest.)
Ah, I've been struck! The blow, alas… is fatal!
(He falls – magnificently.)

PERCINET, *running to Sylvette:*
Sylvette!

SYLVETTE:
My saviour!
(A pretty stage picture of Sylvette in the sedan chair and Percinet on his knees before her. Pasquinot emerges.)

PASQUINOT:
What? Young Bergamin?
Your saviour? Was it *he* who rescued you?
Then – I must offer him your hand in marriage.

SYLVETTE *and* PERCINET:
Good heavens!
(Bergamin has entered from his side, followed by valets with torches.)

PASQUINOT, *to Bergamin, who appears on the crest of the wall:*
Bergamin, your son's a hero!…
Forgive me – and let's make our children happy!

BERGAMIN, *solemnly:*
My hatred's gone.

PERCINET, *softly:*
Sylvette, we must be dreaming!
Let's keep our voices low, lest we awaken!

BERGAMIN:
Feuds always end in marriage; peace is made.
(Indicating the wall:)
This wall exists no more!

PERCINET:
Who would have thought my father capable of such a change?

SYLVETTE, *simply:*
I've always said we'd have a happy ending!
(As they go upstage with Pasquinot, Straforel rises and hands a piece of paper to Bergamin.)

BERGAMIN, *in a low voice:*
For me? A letter, signed by you?

STRAFOREL, *with a bow:*
My bill, sir!

(He falls again, as does the…)

Curtain.

Act Two

The scene is the same, but the wall is no longer there. The benches that were next to it have been pushed to the right and left. There are a few minor changes: flower beds, trellis pavilions, pretentious sculptures of imitation marble, a greenhouse. On the right there is a garden table with chairs.

When the curtain rises, Pasquinot, sitting on the bench on the left side, is reading his gazette. In the background a gardener is raking.

THE GARDENER:
So, Mr Pasquinot, the notary
will come this afternoon? High time, I'd say!
It's been a month now since the wall came down
and all of you've been living here together.
I'm sure our little sweethearts will be happy!

PASQUINOT, *raising his head and looking around:*
Without the wall it's nicer, don't you think?

THE GARDENER:
Oh, yes, it's grand!

PASQUINOT:
          My garden's much improved –
it's twice as handsome.
(He bends down and feels a tuft of grass.)
          Say, this grass is wet!
You watered it – this morning?
(Furious:)
          You old fool!
I told you, water only after sunset!

THE GARDENER, *placidly:*
But Mr Bergamin gave me the order…

PASQUINOT:
Oh? Good old Bergamin – and his fixation!
He thinks that watering constantly is better
than watering sparsely but judiciously!
Well!...
(To the gardener:)
>Go and fetch the plants out of the greenhouse.
(The gardener fetches plants from the greenhouse and lines them up upstage. Pasquinot reads. Bergamin appears upstage with a huge watering can.)

BERGAMIN, *watering the shrubs:*
Oh, dear! They've not been watered nearly enough.
What they require is lots and lots to drink!
(To a tree:)
Hey, friend, are you sheer perishing of thirst?
Here, have a drink – or two!... I love the trees!
(Putting down his watering can, and looking around with satisfaction:)
Oh yes, my garden looks much better now.
I like these imitation-marble sculptures.
(Noticing Pasquinot:)
Hello.
(No reply.)
>Hello!
(Still no reply.)
>>Hello, I said!
(Pasquinot raises his head.)
>>>I'm waiting!

PASQUINOT:
But, friend, we see each other all the time!

BERGAMIN, *indignant:*
Well!...
(Seeing the plants that the gardener is arranging; irritably:)
>Put those plants back, will you?

(The gardener, bewildered, hastily takes them back into the greenhouse. Pasquinot raises his eyes to the sky, shrugs his shoulders and reads. Bergamin walks up and down listlessly and finally sits down next to Pasquinot. Silence. Then, in a fit of melancholy:)

             Every day
at this time I would sneak out of the house…

    PASQUINOT, dreamily, lowering his gazette:
And so would I, on tiptoe, furtively…
What fun it was!

        BERGAMIN:
       The mystery!

        PASQUINOT:
            The danger!

        BERGAMIN:
We had to put the children off the scent
whenever we came out to have a chat.

        PASQUINOT:
And every time we climbed the wall we risked
a broken thigh bone or a fractured rib.

        BERGAMIN:
Our daily colloquies necessitated
finesse and stealth.

        PASQUINOT:
      We had to slip through shrubs…
What fun it was!

        BERGAMIN:
      Some evenings, after crawling
through grass, I'd find my trouser knees were green!

        PASQUINOT:
We always had to swear each other's downfall!

BERGAMIN:
And curse each other out!

PASQUINOT:
What fun it was!

(Yawning:)
Oh, Bergamin!

BERGAMIN, likewise yawning:
Yes, Pasquinot?

PASQUINOT:
We miss it.

BERGAMIN:
No!… Really?
(After reflection:)
Yes, you're right… Hmm. Could this be Romanticism taking its revenge?
(Silence. He looks at Pasquinot, who is reading. Aside:)
There's still that button missing from his waistcoat! That irks me!
(He gets up, walks away, paces up and down.)

PASQUINOT, looking at him over his gazette, aside:
He looks like some giant beetle, with coattails where his forewings ought to be!
(He pretends to read when Bergamin passes by him again.)

BERGAMIN, looking at him, aside:
His eyes cross when he reads, just like a jester watching the bells that dangle from his cap!
(He goes upstage, whistling.)

PASQUINOT, aside, irritated:
That whistling! Such a nervous quirk of his!
(Aloud:)
Stop hissing like an asp!

BERGAMIN, smiling:
You see the mote
that's in your brother's eye, but fail to see
the beam that's in your own? *You* have your quirks!

PASQUINOT:
Who, I?

BERGAMIN:
Yes, you! You waddle like a duck,
you sniffle endlessly – your stopped-up nose
is always black with useless sneezing powder –
and never do you tell a story once,
without repeating it a hundred times.

PASQUINOT, sitting cross-legged and swinging his foot:
But…

BERGAMIN:
Can't you sit two seconds without letting
your foot swing like some massive incense burner?…
And must you roll your breadcrumbs into pellets?
If either one of us is manic, *you* are!

PASQUINOT:
Now that we're bored to death, you've got the leisure
to itemise and catalogue my quirks.
But life together is a great optician,
and now I, too, can see you as you are.
I find you selfish, miserly and false,
with all your petty failings magnified –
just as a harmless little bug becomes
a monstrous beast when seen beneath a lens.

BERGAMIN:
My first suspicion turned out to be true.

PASQUINOT:
Namely?

BERGAMIN:
The wall improved your character.

PASQUINOT:
You lose a lot as well without the wall.

BERGAMIN:
You've stilled my urge to see you every day.

PASQUINOT, bursting out:
For this past month my life's not been worth living!

BERGAMIN, with great dignity:
All right, that's quite enough, sir! What we did
was not for us now, was it?

PASQUINOT:
                         No. Of course not.

BERGAMIN:
But for our children.

PASQUINOT, with conviction:
                     For our children. Yes.
So let us suffer silently, enduring
our loss of freedom with no signs of strain.

BERGAMIN:
For self-denial is the fate of parents.
(Sylvette and Percinet appear on the left, in the background, among the trees, and cross the stage, entwined, with gestures of exaltation.)

PASQUINOT:
Shh! Here they are – the lovers.

BERGAMIN, looking at them:
                      How they pose!
Such attitudes of self-glorification!

PASQUINOT:
Since their adventure satisfied their wishes,

they sense the haloes glowing round their hair!

BERGAMIN:
At this hour daily, in languid attitudes,
like those of lovers in a woodland painting,
they come in reverence to the place of combat
to pay their due respects.
(Sylvette and Percinet, who have disappeared to the right, reappear further downstage and come forward.)
                              Here come our pilgrims.

PASQUINOT:
If they embroider on their usual theme,
it will be well worth listening to.
(Bergamin and Pasquinot withdraw behind a clump of trees and remain hidden.)

PERCINET:
                              I love you!

SYLVETTE:
I love you!
(They stand still.)
                Here it is, the illustrious place.

PERCINET:
Yes, this is where it happened. Here the villain
whom I transpierced collapsed so heavily.

SYLVETTE:
Yes, there was I Andromeda!

PERCINET:
                              I, Perseus!

SYLVETTE:
How many men were there against you?

PERCINET:
                                  Ten.

SYLVETTE:
Oh, surely twenty! Not to count that last one,
whose contumacious humour you corrected.

PERCINET:
I think you're right; they must have numbered thirty.

SYLVETTE:
Tell me again how you – my champion! –
with sword in hand and flaming eyes, subdued them.

PERCINET:
I lunged in fourth – or was it sixth? – position.
No matter; they all fell like dominoes.

SYLVETTE:
If you'd had darker hair, I should have thought
that I was witnessing El Cid in action.

PERCINET:
It's true, we look alike.

SYLVETTE:
What's lacking now
is that our tale of love be set to verse.

PERCINET:
And so it shall!

SYLVETTE:
I love you!

PERCINET:
I love *you*!

SYLVETTE:
A dream come true!… I'd made myself a promise
that I should marry a great romantic hero,
and not the usual humdrum family friend.

PERCINET:
Oh?

Sylvette:
Yes, the type that every girl gets offered –
the timid soul whose sister wants him married,
perhaps some worthy clergyman or other…

Percinet:
Above all, you would never have agreed
– I hope! – to wed the inevitable son
of some good friend of Pasquinot's?

Sylvette, laughing:
                      Oh, no!…

Say, have you noticed lately that our fathers
have been – ill-humoured?

Percinet:
        Yes – irascible.

Bergamin, hidden:
Hmph!

Percinet:
I know why their humour's altered.

Bergamin, hidden:
                      Oh?

Percinet:
The heights we've reached offend their earthbound nature.
Although I've great respect for both our fathers,
they're middle-class and can't live up to us;
our brilliance relegates them to the shadows.

Pasquinot, hidden:
What?

Sylvette:
Now they're just the famous lovers' fathers.

Percinet, laughing:
My great *panache* makes them uncomfortable!

Sylvette, laughing:
When he's with you, your father looks embarrassed,
as if he were – forgive me, may I say it?

Percinet:
You may, you naughty thing!

Sylvette:
As if he were –
a duck discovering that it's hatched an eagle!

Bergamin, hidden:
Ho, ho!

Sylvette, laughing louder:
Poor fathers! Our clandestine love –
what nincompoops it made of them!

Pasquinot, hidden:
Hey, hey!

Percinet:
Of course! For Fate will always join two lovers
by often unforeseen, meandering routes,
and Chance will always play the Figaro
uniting Almaviva and Rosina.

Bergamin, hidden:
Ha, ha!

Sylvette:
And so, this evening we shall sign
our marriage vows!

Percinet, going upstage:
I'll fetch the violins.

Sylvette:
Go quickly, then!

Percinet:
I shan't be gone a moment!

SYLVETTE, calling him back:
No, better still, I'll walk you to the gate.
(They go upstage entwined, Sylvette simpering.)
You know, I really think we are the equals
of all the famous lovers in the legends.

PERCINET:
Yes, we shall take our place among the immortals:
with Romeo and Juliet, of course;
Petrarch and Laura...

SYLVETTE:
Hero and Leander!

PERCINET:
With Pyramus and Thisbe...

SYLVETTE:
Yes! Like us,
they had a wall between them!
(They have gone out. Their voices can be heard receding among the trees.)

PERCINET'S VOICE:
With Francesca
da Rimini and Paolo Malatesta...

SYLVETTE'S VOICE:
With Tristan and Isolde...

BERGAMIN, coming out from behind the trees:
Are you finished?
(Pasquinot emerges as well.)

PASQUINOT, mockingly:
My clever friend, your plan's a wild success,
surpassing all your hopes! Had you foreseen
the outcome – that our children would go mad?

BERGAMIN:
Clearly your daughter's grown most irritating –

with endless boasting of her famed abduction.

PASQUINOT:
The airs your son puts on since he imagines
himself a hero grate on me as well.

BERGAMIN:
But worst of all is how they speak of us,
as two good middle-class buffoons, too stupid
and blind to catch them in a rendezvous.
It's trifling, if you like, but it annoys me.

PASQUINOT:
Had you foreseen that too, my clever friend?
Because of you, your sprat has grown so vain
he takes a bow whenever he hears thunder.

BERGAMIN:
I grant you, his conceit's infuriating.

PASQUINOT:
I'll tell them everything, without delay.

BERGAMIN:
No, don't – not till we've got them safely married;
until the wedding's over, mum's the word!

PASQUINOT:
All right – but now we're tangled in the web
of your ingenious plan!

BERGAMIN:
     My friend, you *liked* it!

PASQUINOT:
A fine plan *that* was!

BERGAMIN, aside:
     How he gets my goat!

(Sylvette enters gaily, a flowering branch in her hand, with which she waves to Percinet, whom she has just left in the wings; she then comes downstage between the two fathers.)

SYLVETTE:
Good morning, dear Papa! Good morning, dear
Papa-in-Law-To-Be!

BERGAMIN:
                      The same to you,
Daughter-in-Law-To-Be!

SYLVETTE, *imitating him:*
                      'The same to you,
Daughter-in-Law-To-Be!' You sound so grumpy
this morning!

BERGAMIN:
It's that Pasquinot, who…

SYLVETTE, *waving her branch in his face:*
                                  Pshht!
Be calm! I come as Peace, with palm in hand!
Are you still sulking? Oh, I quite forgive you!
But can't you two get on like two old friends?

PASQUINOT, *aside:*
The irony!

BERGAMIN, *aloud, sardonically:*
                    It's true; such was our hatred
that now we find it difficult…

SYLVETTE:
                              Just think –
a mortal hatred! Oh, when I remember
the things you used to say about Papa
so often – there, among your lovely roses –
without suspecting I heard everything,
seated behind the wall…

BERGAMIN, aside:
                    Dim-witted girl!

SYLVETTE:
… because I came here every day to meet
with Percinet!
(To Pasquinot:)
                    And when I think that *you*
had no suspicions either…

PASQUINOT, ironically:
                    Never! None!

SYLVETTE:
… although we met the same time every day!
(Laughing, to Bergamin:)
I still can hear how Percinet exclaimed
– remember, on the day of my abduction? –
that he would marry so romantically
that one could never read in any novel
of anything more hopelessly romantic!
By golly, you'll admit he's kept his word!

BERGAMIN, irritated:
Oh, yes?… D'you really think that if I'd wanted…?

SYLVETTE:
Tut-tut! I've read it in a hundred books
that lovers' dreams invariably come true
and fathers in the end grow tenderhearted,
constrained by some improbable event
that forces them eventually to yield.

PASQUINOT:
That forces them to yield? Don't make me laugh!

SYLVETTE:
Haven't we proved it?

BERGAMIN:
               If I were to tell you…

SYLVETTE:

What?

BERGAMIN:

Nothing.

SYLVETTE, to Bergamin:
Why're you being so elusive?

BERGAMIN:

Because I…
(Aside:)
           Ho! It's getting on my nerves!

PASQUINOT:

If I were to reveal…
(Retreating:)
                   No, I'll say nothing.

SYLVETTE:
With nothing to reveal, you have no choice.

PASQUINOT, bursting out:
With nothing to reveal? Child, are you raving?
D'you honestly believe that things can happen
the way they happened? That a sturdy gate
does not protect a garden from invasion?

BERGAMIN:
D'you think that girls get kidnapped nowadays?

SYLVETTE:
Do I think…? What does he mean?

BERGAMIN, losing his temper:
                     I mean: enough!
It's time to let the cat out of the bag!
Oh, yes, since immemorial times, success

has always gone exclusively to youngsters;
for instance, nasty old Don Bartolo
was forced to bow to Almaviva's will.
But now the hour of triumph and revenge
has tolled at last – for those no longer young!

SYLVETTE:

But…

PASQUINOT:

Agèd fathers of the old *commedia
dell'arte* – all so easily deceived –
are no more to be found among us moderns;
the dupes of olden days are now the dupers!
If we had ordered you and Percinet
to fall in love, you wouldn't have obeyed us;
therefore we tricked you – made you fall in love
by cleverly forbidding you to do so.

SYLVETTE:

You mean, you knew?

PASQUINOT:

Of course.

SYLVETTE:

Our tête-à-têtes?

BERGAMIN:

I eavesdropped on your whisperings.

SYLVETTE:

And the benches
we climbed?

PASQUINOT:

… were placed expressly there – by us.

SYLVETTE:

The duel?

Bergamin:
… was merely pantomimed.

Sylvette:
The swordsmen?

Pasquinot:
… were actors.

Sylvette:
My abduction?… No, it *can't* be!

Bergamin, digging into his pocket:
Oh, no? But take a look, I've got the bill –
right here, Miss!

Sylvette, snatching it from him:
Let me see that!
(She reads:)
'Straforel –
A Firm You Trust. One counterfeit abduction,
performed to effectuate a pair's betrothal…'
Oh!… 'Eight dark cloaks at fifteen francs apiece,
eight masks…'

Bergamin, to Pasquinot:
My friend, I think we spoke too soon!

Sylvette, reading:
'An elegant sedan chair with pink cushions,
the latest model…'
(Aloud, ironically:)
So! They do things right!
(She laughs and tosses the bill onto the table.)

Pasquinot, surprised:
You aren't angry?

Sylvette, with good grace:
No! The joke is charming!
But surely it's a lot of wit for nothing.

Dear Mr Bergamin, d'you really think
your subterfuge is why I love your son?

     PASQUINOT, to Bergamin:
She took it well!

     BERGAMIN, to Sylvette:
    You've taken it quite well!

     PASQUINOT:
Can we tell Percinet, then?

     SYLVETTE, quickly:
       No! You mustn't!…
(Recovering:)
Not yet. You know how foolish men can be.

     BERGAMIN:
What good sense! What a clever little head!
And here I thought…
(He pulls out his watch.)
     Excuse me, but… the contract.
We must get ready.
(Holding out his hand to Sylvette:)
     Are we friends?

     SYLVETTE, taking his hand:
       Of course.

  BERGAMIN, turning round again before leaving:
You aren't angry with me?

     SYLVETTE, pure honey:
       Not at all!
(Pasquinot and Bergamin leave. Sylvette, with cold rage:)
How I detest that dreadful Bergamin!

    PERCINET, entering, beaming:
Ah, you're still here?… Of course. I understand.
You just can't bring yourself to leave the spot
where our unheard-of incident took place.

SYLVETTE, sitting on the bench on the left:
Unheard-of, yes.

PERCINET:
It was from there that you,
half swooning, saw me battling like d'Artagnan
those thirty swordsmen…

SYLVETTE:
There were only ten.

PERCINET, coming closer:
My dear, what is it? Why d'you look so sad?
Those sapphires melting into amethysts
that are your eyes seem clouded by *ennui*.

SYLVETTE, aside:
His language is at times a bit pretentious.

PERCINET:
Ah! Now I understand why this fair site
awakes in you such troublesome regrets:
you mourn for our old vine-enshrouded wall,
which once was witness to our hopes and fears.
But it's not been destroyed; it's been exalted,
like Juliet's balcony, to glory…

SYLVETTE, aside, losing her patience:
Ohh!

PERCINET:
… which, ever white, allows its changeless ladder
– gilded by an immortal dawn – to tremble
forever in an endless breeze… beside
a never-wilting pomegranate tree!

SYLVETTE, aside:
Ohh!

PERCINET, ever more lyrical:
Like the eternal lovers in Verona,

we too have made our *mise-en-scène* eternal!
That's why our wall, although torn down, still stands,
and on it grows, like spreading pellitory,
our admirable love!

Sylvette, aside:
             He does go on!

Percinet, with a meaningful smile:
But it was you, who hoped just now to see
a poem rhymed about our story… Well,
that poem…

Sylvette, uneasy:
   Yes?

Percinet:
   I'm rhyming it myself!

Sylvette:
Can you write verse?

Percinet:
   Did I know how to fence?
Here's the beginning, which I've just composed:
'Two Hostile Fathers', narrative in verse.

Sylvette:
Ohh!

Percinet, assuming a declamatory pose:
   Strophe one.

Sylvette:
Ohh!

Percinet:
    What's the matter?

Sylvette:
               Nothing –
just happiness… or nerves… a spell of weakness…

(She melts into tears.)
I'll be all right, just leave me for a moment.
(Seated on the bench, she turns her back on him and hides her face in her handkerchief.)

PERCINET, *momentarily stunned:*
I'll leave you then.
(Then, aside, with a superior smile:)
On such a day her upset
is natural.
(He goes to the right, sees a piece of paper lying on the table, pulls a pencil from his pocket and sits down.)
I must write down my verses.
(He picks up the paper and is about to write on it, but stops, pencil raised, and reads:)
'Whereas I, Straforel, contrived to fall
as if an unskilled blade had run me through,
I assess for damage to my garb ten francs;
for damage to my self-esteem, one hundred.'
(Smiling:)
What's this, then?
(As he continues reading silently, his smile fades and his eyes grow wide.)

SYLVETTE, *aside, still on the bench, wiping her eyes:*
He'd be crushed if he found out.
I nearly gave myself away. Sylvette,
be careful!

PERCINET, *getting up:*
Ho!... Oho!

SYLVETTE, *turning towards him:*
What did you say?

PERCINET, *quickly hiding the bill in his pocket:*
Er – nothing!

SYLVETTE, aside:
His delusion saddens me.

PERCINET, aside:
So that's why no one ever found the body!

SYLVETTE, aside, getting up:
He's sulking, so it seems. I'll talk to him.
(She turns this way and that for a moment, as if showing off her dress; then, seeing that he does not react, she says coquettishly:)
You haven't said a word about my frock?

PERCINET, negligently:
Blue's not your colour. Pink would suit you better.

SYLVETTE, aside, startled:
Blue's not my colour?... Has he since found out?
(Panicked, looking at the table:)
The bill! I know I must have left it there!

PERCINET, seeing her turning round, searching:
Why are you twirling round like that?

SYLVETTE, aloud:
                                               No reason!

(Aside:)
The wind may well have taken it.
(Aloud, expressly turning round to make her skirt billow:)
                                               No reason!
I twirled to see how well this fashion suits me!...
(Aside:)
Might he have found it? I'll find out for sure...
(Aloud:)
Um – you were just about to speak some verses
about our tale of love?
(Percinet winces. She takes his arm and says, very gently:)
                                      I'd like to hear them.

PERCINET:
Oh, no.

SYLVETTE:
Yes, please! Recite your verses.

PERCINET:
No.

SYLVETTE, ironically:
The 'narrative in verse' of our adventure!

PERCINET:
They didn't suit… They didn't fit…

SYLVETTE:
… the bill?

PERCINET:
What? Fit the bill?
(Startled, he looks at her.)
Excuse me, but…

SYLVETTE:
I'm sorry!

PERCINET, aside:
Oh. Then she knows?

SYLVETTE, aside:
He knows, then?

BOTH, together:
So you know?
(A moment, then they both burst out laughing.)

PERCINET:
That's very funny, don't you think?

SYLVETTE:
Yes, very!

PERCINET:
They certainly made fools of us!

SYLVETTE:

Indeed!

PERCINET:
Our fathers were good friends?

SYLVETTE:

And more – good neighbours!

PERCINET:
Who knows? They might have even been first cousins!

SYLVETTE, with a curtsy:
I'm marrying my cousin!

PERCINET, bowing:

So am I!

SYLVETTE:
How sweet!

PERCINET:
How classic!

SYLVETTE:

Surely one could think
of more romantic matches, but… how pleasant,
that love and duty could be reconciled!

PERCINET:
And property! Their gardens, their estates…

SYLVETTE:
In short, a classic marriage of convenience.
How far from our poor idyll on the wall!

PERCINET:
No, one can't speak of idylls any more!

SYLVETTE:
I'm back to being just an average girl.

PERCINET:
And I'm the normal little 'groom next door'.
Yet – Romeo was the role in which I pleased you!

SYLVETTE:
Ah, Romeo! Clearly you're no longer he!

PERCINET:
D'you really think that you're still Juliet?

SYLVETTE:
You're turning bitter.

PERCINET:
      Ho! You're turning acid.

SYLVETTE:
If you appeared ridiculous – my God! –
is that my fault?

PERCINET:
      Well, if in fact I did,
I wasn't all alone.

SYLVETTE:
      All right, we *both* did!…
Ah, my poor bluebird, how your plumes have faded!

PERCINET, jeering:
Your sham abduction!

SYLVETTE:
      Your factitious swordfight!

PERCINET:
A kidnapping for show!

SYLVETTE:
      A bogus rescue!
Our poetry was but a laughingstock!
Now that the iridescent bubble's burst
before our startled eyes, there's nothing left

but soapy water raining on our noses!

      PERCINET:
O Romeo, how deplorably I mimed you!
O Juliet, how unworthy was your actress!
With Shakespeare's noble couple we had nothing
at all in common…

      SYLVETTE:
      Absolutely nothing!

      PERCINET:
We didn't play the Bard's supernal drama,
we mocked it in a shameful parody!

      SYLVETTE:
Our nightingale was just a common bullfinch.

      PERCINET:
Our everlasting wall, a puppet theatre.
And when we went there every day to meet,
appearing from the rib cage up, we weren't
two paragons of endless love, but puppets
that fat paternal fingers brought to life!

      SYLVETTE:
That's true. But we'd become still more absurd,
were that to make us love each other less.

      PERCINET:
Let's love each other, then, with wild abandon –
since we must love each other anyway.

      SYLVETTE:
But we adore each other!

      PERCINET:
      Yes, we do –
the word is not too strong!

Sylvette:
                    And love can offer
great consolation after such misfortune.
Don't you agree, my precious?

Percinet:
                              Yes, my treasure.

Sylvette:
Goodbye, my dearest heart!

Percinet:
                        Adieu, my beauty!

Sylvette:
I'll dream of you, belovèd – on my side.

Percinet:
And I of you on mine. Goodbye!

Sylvette:
                                   Adieu!

(She goes out.)

Percinet:
Imagine that – that I should be so treated!…
(He notices Straforel entering upstage.)
But who can this moustachioed stranger be,
whose ample cloak reveals a curious doublet?…
(Straforel majestically comes downstage. Percinet addresses him.)
What is it?

Straforel, smiling:
It concerns a modest sum.

Percinet:
A tradesman?

Straforel:
Yes, exactly. Go, young man,

and tell your father that I'm here.

PERCINET:

Your name?

STRAFOREL:

I'm Straforel.

PERCINET, starting:

No!… Straforel? You, here?
It isn't to be borne!

STRAFOREL, smiling:

Aha! They've told you!

PERCINET, pulling the crumpled bill from his pocket and throwing it at him:

You wretch! 'Twas you!

STRAFOREL:
'Twas I, indeed, by Jove!

PERCINET, aside:
To find this brute I would have searched the world!

STRAFOREL, amused, self-satisfied:
The man you killed is in the pink of health!

PERCINET, rushing at him with sword in hand:
I'll show you!

STRAFOREL, parrying with his arm, calm as a fencing-master giving a lesson:
Lift the hand!… Advance the foot!
At your age, to be so unschooled – for shame!
(With a flick of the wrist he disarms Percinet and, bowing, offers him his sword back.)
What? Tired already of your fencing lesson?

PERCINET, humiliated, taking his sword back:
I'll leave, then – as I'm treated like a child!
But I'll have my revenge! I'll know romance –

for real! And with my countless loves and duels
I'll sweep away the memory of Don Juan!…
I'll kidnap ladies of the theatre!
(He runs out, brandishing his sword.)

STRAFOREL.

Fine.
But now the question is: will I get paid?
(Looking into the wings and calling out:)
Hey! Break it up, you two!… Another scuffle!
(Enter Bergamin and Pasquinot, dishevelled, tattered, as if after a fight.)

PASQUINOT, *adjusting himself and giving Bergamin his hairpiece back:*
Here, take your hairpiece!

BERGAMIN:
Oof! And you, take yours!

PASQUINOT:
You understand that after such behaviour…
Here, take your collar!

BERGAMIN:
Surely you must see
that life with you would be a sacrifice
I will not make – not even for my son!
(Sylvette enters.)

PASQUINOT, *seeing Sylvette:*
Sylvette!… She mustn't learn of this!

SYLVETTE, *throwing her arms around her father's neck:*
Papa,
I *will* no longer marry Percinet!
(The notary enters for the signing of the contract with four citizens dressed in their Sunday best as witnesses.)

BERGAMIN:
The notary! The witnesses!… Oh, damn!

THE NOTARY, *stunned:*
Such language!

TWO OF THE WITNESSES, *with offended dignity:*
Really!

STRAFOREL, *in the middle of the tumult, holding up the bill thrown at him by Percinet:*
Ninety gold pistoles –
I insist you pay my bill!
(Several guests enter, as well as three violinists playing a minuet.)

BERGAMIN, *beside himself, jostling the new arrivals:*
The violins!…
Oh, damn!
(The violins automatically continue their minuet.)

STRAFOREL, *impatiently, holding out his hand, to Bergamin:*
I'm waiting!

BERGAMIN:
Speak to Pasquinot!
(Straforel turns to Pasquinot.)

PASQUINOT:
Ask Bergamin!
(Straforel turns again to Bergamin.)

STRAFOREL, *quoting the words of his bill:*
'One counterfeit abduction, performed to effectuate a pair's betrothal…'

BERGAMIN:
They're *un*betrothed – so I don't have to pay!

STRAFOREL, *turning to Pasquinot:*
But you, sir…

PASQUINOT:
Not one sou – our plans are ruined!
(The gardener has entered and whispered something to Bergamin.)

BERGAMIN:
My son's – run off?

SYLVETTE, *startled:*
Run off?
(Straforel, on his way upstage, stops at her reaction and turns to look at her.)

STRAFOREL:
Well, fancy that!

BERGAMIN:
Quick, we must find him! After him!
(He runs out, followed by the notary, the witnesses and the guests.)

SYLVETTE, *deeply affected:*
Run off!

STRAFOREL, *coming back downstage, still watching her:*
If I could only reunite the lovebirds,
perhaps I could…

SYLVETTE:
Run off?
(Suddenly furious:)
Oh, that's the limit!
(She storms out, followed by Pasquinot.)

STRAFOREL, *undefeated:*
Well, Straforel, my lad, to get your shekels,
you'll have to patch this union back together!
(He goes out. The three violinists, left alone in the middle of the stage, continue playing their minuet.)

Curtain.

Act Three

The same setting. Materials have been brought in for the reconstruction of the wall, which has begun at the back: bags of plaster, a wheelbarrow, troughs and trowels.

When the curtain rises, a mason is working, crouched down with his back to the audience. Bergamin and Pasquinot, each on his own side, are inspecting the work.

THE MASON, *singing while working:*
'Deh vieni alla finestra...'[1]

BERGAMIN:
Oh, how slowly these masons work!

THE MASON:
'... o mio teso-oro.'

PASQUINOT, *following his movements with satisfaction:*
Aah! Now he puts the rubble stones in mortar!

BERGAMIN, *likewise:*
Aah! Now he spreads the mortar...

PASQUINOT:
... with his trowel!

THE MASON, *with lyrical grandeur:*
'Deh vieni a consolar il pianto mio.'

PASQUINOT, *coming downstage:*
Impressive voice! Too bad his work's so slow!

BERGAMIN, *also coming downstage, with aggressive pleasure:*
A fragment of the wall's begun already!

PASQUINOT, *indicating with his foot the place not yet built:*
Tomorrow, by this time, it will have risen

---

[1] Don Giovanni's serenade from Mozart's opera.

a good two feet above the ground – hurrah!

BERGAMIN, lyrically:
Dear wall, may I soon see you stand again!

PASQUINOT:
What's that, sir?

BERGAMIN:
I was not addressing you.
(A pause.)
What do you do now after dinner?

PASQUINOT:
Nothing.

And you, sir?

BERGAMIN:
Er – not much of anything.
(A pause. They bow and wander about.)

PASQUINOT, stopping:
There's no news of your son, then?

BERGAMIN:
Not a word.
Still running wild.

PASQUINOT, politely:
The gentle sex will quickly deplete him of his money; then, of course, he'll come back home at once.

BERGAMIN, politely:
You're very kind.
(They bow again and continue walking. A pause.)

PASQUINOT, stopping:
Now that the wall is rising, sir, I'd gladly receive you on occasion – as a neighbour.

BERGAMIN:
All right. Perhaps I'll honour you…
(They bow to each other.)

PASQUINOT, abruptly:
Oh, do!
An evening of piquet?

BERGAMIN, stammering:
Er – I'm not sure if…

PASQUINOT:
But you're invited!

BERGAMIN, flustered:
Lord!…
(Having made his decision:)
But not piquet; let's play bezique.

PASQUINOT:
Come on, then!

BERGAMIN, going out after him:
You still owe me ten sous from last time.
(Turning round:)
Carry on, dear mason!

THE MASON, at the top of his voice:
'Fin ch'han dal vino…'[2]

PASQUINOT:
What a glorious voice!
(They leave. As soon as they are gone, the mason turns round and takes off his hat; it is Straforel.)

STRAFOREL:
Yes, I'm the mason – come here in disguise,

---

[2] Don Giovanni's so-called 'Champagne Aria'.

because I've some replastering to do!
(Sitting on the rebuilt portion of the wall:)
The young man's still pursuing his 'romance';
one needs no crystal ball to prophesy
that he'll return with empty hands and heart.
And so, while life itself assumes the task
of de-naivifying our naïf
by giving him a salutary dunking
and sending him back home on drooping wings,
I, in a clever parallel manoeuvre,
am working here to cure Sylvette of leanings
to adventure… Often, in the provinces,
the multitalented young Straforel
played marquesses and princes on the stage –
to catcalls from the unenlightened public.
The expertise I gained there will be useful.
(He pulls a letter from his smock and puts it in the mossy opening of a tree trunk.)
Oh, Pasquinot and Bergamin, how thankful
you'll be to me!
(He sees Sylvette entering; she is wearing a diaphanous veil over her shoulders.)
    She's here!… To my cement!
(He returns to his plastering and disappears behind the wall. Sylvette comes in, furtively, looking about to see if she is being observed.)

    SYLVETTE:

No, no one!
(She places her veil on the bench, left.)
    Is a letter here for me?
(She goes towards the tree in which Straforel has deposited his letter.)
An unknown cavalier comes every day
to place a letter for me in this tree trunk,
once cleft by lightning – now a sylvan postbox.

(Plunging her arm into the hollow of the tree:)
Yes, here's my post.
(She reads:)
'Sylvette, marmoreal heart!
I'll write no more, you tigress! Though I *ply* you
with love notes every day, you don't *re-ply.*'
Hoo! What a style! 'Love, rumbling in my soul…'
(She nervously crumples the letter.)
Ohh!… Percinet's gone out to see the world –
and rightly so! I want to do the same!
Or must I stay at home and die of boredom?
Let him appear – the man who writes these letters!
Should he materialise behind those shrubs,
I wouldn't even go to fetch a hat;
just as I am, I'd follow him, right now!
Romance at any cost! Let him appear –
already I'm well-nigh in love with him!
I'd hold out both my hands to him in welcome…

  STRAFOREL, *appearing, in a thundering voice:*
He's here!

     SYLVETTE:
 Help! Percinet!
(He advances upon her; with his every step, she backs one step away from him.)
      Sir, keep your distance!

    STRAFOREL, *amorously:*
But why so hostile? After all, I'm he
whose style you so admired, the favoured mortal
whose letter pleased you so, and on whose love
you counted – if your words can be believed –
to have you kidnapped and to flee with you
beyond the reach of anyone.

    SYLVETTE, *at a complete loss:*
      But – you!

Straforel:
You thought I was a mason? How exquisite!
May I present myself? I am the Marquess
of Astafiorquercita – mad in spirit,
but sick at heart. An all-too-bland existence
I seek to spice by travelling the world –
knight-errant, bard and dreamer, all in one!
It was to invade your garden, cruel creature,
for love of you, that I took up the trowel!
(He tosses his trowel away with an elegant gesture and quickly removes his smock and his plaster-whitened hat, revealing a dazzling nobleman's costume, complete with blond wig and swaggering moustache.)

Sylvette:
Oh, sir!

Straforel:
A man named Straforel apprised me
of your sad story, and a frenzied love
took hold of me – for you, the innocent,
dazed victim of that ignominious plot.

Sylvette:
But, Marquess…

Straforel:
No, you needn't look so frightened –
for when he boasted of his scurvy role,
I killed him.

Sylvette:
Killed him?

Straforel:
With a single sword-blow.
I've always been a passionate avenger.

Sylvette:
But, sir…

STRAFOREL:
I understand your misjudged heart.
You want romance at any cost?

SYLVETTE:
But, Marquess!

STRAFOREL:
It's settled then. I'll kidnap you tonight…

SYLVETTE:
But I…

STRAFOREL:
… this time for real!

SYLVETTE:
But, sir!

STRAFOREL:
Oh joy!
You've given your consent – I heard your words!
This evening we'll begin our headlong flight –
and if it breaks your father's heart, so be it!

SYLVETTE:
But, Marquess, I…

STRAFOREL:
And if they hunt us down
– for kidnappers are doggedly pursued –
so much the better!

SYLVETTE:
But…

STRAFOREL:
So much the better!
If it's a stormy night we'll flee on foot,
our foreheads battered by the wind and rain.

SYLVETTE:
But, sir…

STRAFOREL:
We'll board a ship with all due haste
to reach some distant continent…

SYLVETTE:
But, sir…

STRAFOREL:
… and far away, in some unpeopled land,
we'll live for pleasure – clad in serge and sackcloth.

SYLVETTE:
Oh! But…

STRAFOREL:
For I possess no worldly goods –
you wouldn't want me to!

SYLVETTE:
Well, actually…

STRAFOREL:
Our only meals will be of bread – bread moistened
with sweetest tears!

SYLVETTE:
Nevertheless…

STRAFOREL:
Our exile
will be for us a paradise of charms!

SYLVETTE:
But, sir…

STRAFOREL:
We'll find our fortune in *mis*fortune!
Have I your heart, I'll need no thatch-roofed cottage –
a tent will do.

Sylvette:
A tent?

Straforel:
Four simple poles,
two sheets of canvas… or, if you prefer,
nothing at all – we'll sleep under the stars!

Sylvette:
Oh! But…

Straforel:
What is it? Why're you all atremble?
You'd rather not go quite so far away?
All right… But having outraged public morals,
we'll have to live in hiding, just we two!
Oh ecstasy!

Sylvette:
But, sir, I never meant…

Straforel:
The world will turn from us in scorn…

Sylvette, aside:
Dear God!

Straforel:
… but prejudices must be trodden down,
and we'll *enjoy* the odium of the masses!

Sylvette:
But, sir…

Straforel:
I'll have no occupation other
than telling you at length how I adore you.

Sylvette:
But, sir…

STRAFOREL:
In short, we'll live in poetry!…
I'll have my fits of jealousy, of course…

SYLVETTE:
But, sir…

STRAFOREL:
… and when I'm jealous, I'm as savage
as any jackal, fierce as any wolf.

SYLVETTE, collapsing, crushed, onto the bench:
But, sir…

STRAFOREL:
Were you to break our sacred bond,
I'd execute you on the spot.

SYLVETTE:
But, sir…

STRAFOREL:
You're shaking so!

SYLVETTE, aside:
Oh God! What have I done?

STRAFOREL, thundering:
Great Scott! Do you have blood or porridge coursing
through your arterial vessels? Botheration!
You seem to me a bit too much the schoolgirl
to dare to face so hazardous a future!
I'll go alone, then… Or will you come too?

SYLVETTE:
Please, Marquess…

STRAFOREL, gently:
Ah, my voice has reassured you!
Well, now that you feel strong again, we'll leave.
I'll kidnap you without delay, on horseback,

across my saddle… Oh – that's rather painful,
but… portable sedan chairs, built for comfort,
are never used except in fake abductions!

> SYLVETTE:

But, sir…

> STRAFOREL, *going upstage as if to exit:*
> I'll see you soon!

> SYLVETTE:
> But, sir…

> STRAFOREL:
> Till later!

Now I must go and fetch a horse, a coat…

> SYLVETTE, *beside herself:*

But, sir…

> STRAFOREL, *with a vast gesture:*
> And then – we're off to see the world!

(Coming back downstage:)
Oh, dearest soul – long dreamed of, finally met!
The soul my soul can call a kindred spirit!
I'll see you soon, and then – forevermore!

> SYLVETTE, *in an extinguished voice:*

Forevermore!

> STRAFOREL:
> You'll live beside the lover

for whom you yearned before you ever knew him –
and who, before he knew you, burned for you.
(Before going out, seeing her collapsed on the bench:)
You may come home now, Master Percinet!
(He goes out.)

> SYLVETTE, *opening her eyes, hallucinating:*

Sir?… Marquess?… No! Please, not across the saddle!
Be merciful! I'm not the girl you think –

oh, not at all! Let me go home, I beg you!
I'm just a schoolgirl – as you said!...
(Coming to:)

He's gone!...

Sir?... I'm alone?...
(Now fully awake:)

God, what a ghastly dream!

(A moment. She recovers.)
I'd rather have a make-believe abduction!
(She stands up and smiles ruefully.)
Well, well, Sylvette, my lass! What is it, hmm?
You clamoured for romance – then, when it came,
you weren't happy?... No, the serge and sackcloth,
the tent, the stars, the exile – that's too much!
I wanted just a taste of such romance
– as one might put a bay leaf in the stew –
but not all that! I couldn't stand such jolts.
With gentler feelings I'd be satisfied...
(Twilight subtly comes over the garden. Sylvette picks up her veil from the bench, covers her head and shoulders with it, and says dreamily:)
Who knows if...?
(Percinet appears. He is in rags, his arm in a sling, barely dragging himself along. A felt hat, from which a broken feather hangs pitifully, hides his features.)

PERCINET, *still unseen by Sylvette:*
I've not eaten for two days,
I'm dropping with fatigue – and I'm not proud.
A sorry escapade! I saw hard times;
adventures aren't any fun at all.
(He slumps against the wall. His hat falls, revealing his face. Sylvette sees him.)

SYLVETTE:
You!
(He stands up, startled. She looks at him.)

And in such a state! Can this be true?

PERCINET, piteously:
It can.

SYLVETTE, clasping her hands together:
Good God!

PERCINET:
I must look like a drawing
one might make of *The Prodigal's Return*…
(He staggers.)

SYLVETTE:
You're near collapse!

PERCINET:
I'm rather tired.

SYLVETTE, seeing his arm, with a cry:
You're wounded!

PERCINET, quickly:
Would you be merciful to such an ingrate?

SYLVETTE, sternly, moving away:
Sir, only fathers kill the fatted calf.
(Percinet makes a movement, and his wounded arm causes him to grimace. Sylvette is frightened in spite of herself.)
And yet – your wound…

PERCINET:
Not serious, I assure you.

SYLVETTE:
But what have you been doing all this time,
a vagrant?

PERCINET:
Nothing good at all, Sylvette.
(He coughs.)

SYLVETTE:
You're coughing now?

PERCINET:
Good Lord, I tramped at night along the highways…

SYLVETTE:
… where you caught a chill. What strange clothes you have on!

PERCINET:
Yes. Highwaymen robbed me of mine and left me these – their castoffs.

SYLVETTE, ironically:
How many times did fortune smile on you?

PERCINET:
Sylvette, let's drop these inconvenient questions.

SYLVETTE:
But surely you climbed many a balcony?

PERCINET, aside:
And just as surely almost broke my neck…

SYLVETTE:
You must recall one sweet success or two?

PERCINET, aside:
I spent three days concealed inside a cupboard.

SYLVETTE:
And did you win at least one gallant wager?

PERCINET:
Oh yes!…
(Aside:)
A jealous husband beat me up.

SYLVETTE:
Guitar in hand, you serenaded damsels?

Percinet, aside:
Who oft as not threw crockery at my head.

Sylvette:
At last you fought an actual duel, I see?

Percinet, aside:
Which garnered me this nearly fatal blow.

Sylvette:
Now you've come home?

Percinet:
Exhausted, gaunt, in tatters!

Sylvette.
Yes… but at least you found poetic – glimmers?

Percinet:
No; far I roamed to seek what lay so near.
Don't mock me now, I beg you… I adore you!

Sylvette:
Despite our having been so disillusioned?

Percinet:
What of it?

Sylvette:
But our fathers cruelly tricked us.

Percinet:
What of it? In my heart there's sunlight now.

Sylvette:
They feigned their hatred!

Percinet:
Did we feign our love?

Sylvette:
Our wall was, as you said, a puppet theatre.

PERCINET:
Then what I said was blasphemy... Or was it?
For what a stage our old wall offered us!
With branches framing the proscenium,
a garden view receding in perspective
as backdrop, endless azure sky as fly space,
the breezes as an unseen orchestra,
the flowers as props, the sun to light the stage,
and even William Shakespeare as our prompter!...
Oh yes, our fathers were the puppeteers
whose scheming hands made us perform our gestures;
but on that puppet stage – think back, Sylvette! –
it was our love that made us speak our lines.

SYLVETTE, sighing:
Ah, yes, we loved – but thought our love was sinful.

PERCINET, quickly:
And so it was!... Preserve those pleasant qualms!
Intentions are equivalent to deeds:
believing we were doing wrong, we were!

SYLVETTE, wavering:
You're certain?

PERCINET:
Absolutely, dear Sylvette.
It was a grievous deed that we committed.
I swear by your sweet breath and by your grace,
to love each other as we did was wicked.

SYLVETTE, nearly convinced, sitting down beside him:
Quite wicked?
(Changing her mind, getting up and moving away again:)
That's all well and good – but sadly,
if only for the sake of our renown,
the danger we were in was mere illusion.

Percinet:
No, it was real for us, who thought it real.

Sylvette:
No; my abduction, like your duel, was faked.

Percinet:
Your fear was real, though! Since your state of mind,
Sylvette, was that of someone being kidnapped,
it's just as if they'd kidnapped you for real!

Sylvette:
No… Memories that I'd cherished have been spoilt:
the masks, the cloaks, the torchlight, that soft music,
the swordplay – all the charm, in fact. Too cruel
to think that Straforel produced it all!

Percinet:
Did Straforel produce the April twilight?
Was he the organiser of the party
that springtime kindly threw for us that evening?
Did he dispose the stars? Did he obscure,
with subtle use of shade, the spindly rose shrubs,
so that the blooms themselves appeared to float
uncannily, suspended in mid-air?
The languid atmosphere, was that his doing?
The shimmering blue reflections? Did he hang
the pink and silver moon up in the sky?

Sylvette:
Of course not…

Percinet:
         And did he, on that spring night,
arrange that two young people loved each other?
For *therein,* dear Sylvette, lay all the charm.

Sylvette:
That's true, therein lay all the…
(She falters, momentarily unable to speak.)

But…

PERCINET:
You're weeping?
You've pardoned, then, the nasty runaway?

SYLVETTE:
Poor boy, I've always loved you!

PERCINET:
Once again
I've found your forehead, with its childlike curls,
and your faint perfume, delicately blending
with perfumes from the nearby gold laburnums.
No angel ever knew such bliss as mine!
(He plays with Sylvette's veil.)
Oh, let me kiss the border of your veil,
which floats down like a zephyr from your forehead!
It cools my lips, this gossamer…
(With sudden bitterness:)
… for which
I couldn't scorn deceptive plush and velvets!

SYLVETTE:
What – plush and velvets?

PERCINET, *recovering, quickly:*
Nothing – only rags.
Sylvette, child, muslin is your element.
Oh, how I love this veil!

SYLVETTE:
It's made of linen.

PERCINET:
I love it, but I fear my kiss may taint it;
perhaps it's better just to kneel before it.
(He is about to kneel, but she takes his hands, bidding him rise.)

SYLVETTE:
True poetry lies in the hearts of lovers;
it doesn't emanate from mere – adventures.

PERCINET:
That's true; the adventures I went through, though real,
were not at all poetic, dear Sylvette.

SYLVETTE:
Yet those arranged by our two fathers *were*,
despite not being real, dear Percinet.

PERCINET:
For when we love, our souls can well embroider
real flowers on an imaginary canvas.

SYLVETTE, in his arms:
My love! What fools we were to search abroad
for poetry – when it was in ourselves!
(Straforel reappears, bringing the two fathers with him.)

STRAFOREL, indicating the young couple:
They're rebetrothed!

BERGAMIN:
My son!
(He embraces Percinet.)

STRAFOREL:
You'll pay my bill now?

PASQUINOT, to his daughter:
Once more you love him?

SYLVETTE:
Yes.

PASQUINOT:
Dear, silly child!

STRAFOREL, to Bergamin:
I'll get my gold now?

BERGAMIN:
Every last pistole!

SYLVETTE, *who has started at the sound of Straforel's voice:*
But – wait! I know that voice! The Marquess of…
(Struggling to recall the name:)
… of Asta-… fior-…

STRAFOREL, *with a bow:*
Of Astafiorquercita?
Yes, it was I, dear lady – Straforel!
Forgive my zeal. My method, though, had merit:
it made you aware, while keeping you at home,
of all the tiresome traits of real adventures,
with which most ladies soon grow disenchanted.
No doubt you could have sampled them yourself…
(Indicating Percinet:)
… as this young man did; but as I consider
that method too extreme for a young lady,
I let you see the magic-lantern version.

PERCINET:
What's that he's saying?

SYLVETTE, *quickly:*
Pay no mind! I love you!

BERGAMIN, *indicating the newly begun portion of the wall:*
First thing tomorrow, with a single blow
– bang! – of the pickaxe, we'll tear down this wall…

PASQUINOT:
… removing all that stone, cement and sand!

STRAFOREL:
No, build the wall – it's indispensable!

SYLVETTE, *gathering the other actors around her and addressing the audience:*
We five now offer you our closing rondel

to vindicate the play that you've just seen.
(She steps to the footlights and recites:)
  Bright costumes and verses to hold you in thrall!
  A garden where Cupid's sweet music is played!

    BERGAMIN:
A merry quintet, a naive escapade!

    PASQUINOT:
Some conflicts, of course, but ephemeral and small!

    STRAFOREL:
The sun's golden beams and the moon's silver ball!
A swordsman who sings a renowned serenade!

    SYLVETTE:
Bright costumes and verses to hold you in thrall!
A garden where Cupid's sweet music is played!

    PERCINET:
Respite from such plays that offend or appall:
a pastoral idyll!... We've not overstayed
our welcome, I hope, with our glad masquerade:
two lovers, two fathers, one swordsman, one wall!

    SYLVETTE, *with a curtsy:*
Bright costumes and verses to hold you in thrall!

Curtain.